Video Games and Society

Video Games, Violence, and Crime

Video Games and Society

Video Games, Violence, and Crime

Patricia D. Netzley

ReferencePoint Press®

San Diego, CA

© 2015 ReferencePoint Press, Inc.
Printed in the United States

For more information, contact:
ReferencePoint Press, Inc.
PO Box 27779
San Diego, CA 92198
www.ReferencePointPress.com

LIBRARY OF CONGRESS CATALOGING-IN-PUBLICATION DATA

Netzley, Patricia D.
  Video games, violence, and crime / by Patricia D. Netzley.
     pages cm. — (Video games and society series)
  Includes bibliographical references and index.
  ISBN-13: 978-1-60152-752-3 (hardback)
  ISBN-10: 1-60152-752-7 (hardback)
  1. Violence in video games—Juvenile literature. 2. Video games—Social aspects—Juvenile literature. 3. Violence—Juvenile literature. 4. Crime—Juvenile literature. I. Title.
  GV1469.34.V56N483 2015
  794.8—dc23
                                                        2014019959

Contents

Compelling Violence

When the first home versions of video games appeared in the 1970s and 1980s, few people realized just how popular they would become over the next few decades. In 1982 the revenue of the home video game industry was $3.8 billion; in 2013, according to the Entertainment Software Association (ESA), American consumers spent $21.53 billion on video games, hardware, and accessories. The ESA reports that as of January 2014, 59 percent of Americans play video games, and 71 percent of them are age eighteen or older.

For some of these players, gaming is not a casual hobby but an important part of daily life. More than 60 percent of them play games with others, either in the presence of other players or online, and many of these individuals gain a sense of community from their game play. Some also join clubs devoted to particular games and attend events dressed as their favorite characters. Many positive experiences can come out of such activities. However, they can also create difficulties for gamers who cannot limit the amount of time devoted to them. When people become obsessed with gaming, they can play for so many hours that it destroys their relationships with friends and family, costs them their jobs, and brings financial hardship and depression.

First-Person Shooters

Many of the downsides related to video games are, according to experts, the result of heavy gaming. Some believe that heavy gaming can make people more aggressive and perhaps even violent, particularly if the games being played involve committing violent acts in the world of the game. Ohio State professor of communication and psychology Brad Bushman, who has spent roughly twenty-five years studying the link between violent games and violent behavior, says this is largely because "video games require the player to identify and interact with a violent character instead of just observing them."[1]

One type of video game provides an especially strong connection between the game player and a violent game character: the first-person shooter game. Such games put the player in the point of view of a character who is firing a weapon at other characters. In other words, the player is seeing the action through the eyes of a game character who is killing others. Some first-person shooter games also offer a third-person camera mode, whereby the player is viewing the game from just behind and slightly above the shooter.

These games have millions of players. For example, according to the game company Activision, more than 400 million people play games from its *Call of Duty* franchise each month. As of the end of 2013, this consisted of ten games, and more than 100 million copies of these games have been sold since the first *Call of Duty* was released in 2003. Activision also reports that gamers spent more than 1.6 billion hours playing its *Call of Duty* game *Modern Warfare 3* online between its release in 2011 and the end of 2013.

> "Video games require the player to identify and interact with a violent character instead of just observing them."[1]
>
> —Brad Bushman, *a professor of communication and psychology at Ohio State University.*

Adrenaline Rushes

Lennart Nacke, the director of the Games and Media Entertainment Research Laboratory at the University of Ontario Institute of Technology, says the main reason first-person shooter games are so popular is that they require quick-thinking decisions that provide a kind of excitement most people do not experience in real life. He explains why this is so compelling:

> If you look at it in terms of our evolution, most of us have office jobs. We're in front of the computer all day. We don't have to go out and fight a tiger or a bear to find our dinner. But it's still hardwired in humans. Our brain craves this kind of interaction, our brain wants to be stimulated. We miss this adrenaline-generating decision-making.[2]

A menacing figure in the game Titanfall *is projected on a screen during a promotional preview of the game in 2013. Many believe that the violence in such games is highly addictive to gamers.*

This craving can lead some people to return to the gaming world again and again, which is perhaps why many gamers say that first-person shooter games are highly addictive. Gamer Steve Tilley, for example, reports being addicted to a multiplayer first-person shooter game called *Titanfall*. But it is not just the quick decisions that compel him to play. It is the violence, as evidenced by what he says he longs to do when his desire to play *Titanfall* overtakes him: "I want to sneak up behind an adversary holed up in a sniper's [nest] and snap his neck with a satisfying crack. I want the cheap but rewarding thrill of crushing a group of hapless A.I.-controlled [artificial intelligence–controlled] enemy grunts beneath my Ogre's feet."[3]

Losing Control

People who play such games typically have no problem witnessing and committing violent acts in the game world. But experts say that repeatedly engaging in such violence can desensitize someone to violence in the real world, making that person less likely to be disturbed by real-life brutalities. Studies have shown that heavy gamers can also become desensitized to racism, sexism, and other negative thoughts and behaviors that they have witnessed in the video games they play.

Gamers themselves admit that desensitization is a valid concern. For example, Eric Falascino, who admits to playing video games daily, says, "Violence (in video games) definitely affects the player, to a degree. You get used to seeing violence, and you become more tolerant of it." He adds that game violence might also cause a player to feel some aggression that could spill over into real life. Falascino believes that whether game violence leads to real violence is "all up to self-control."[4]

> "Violence (in video games) definitely affects the player, to a degree. You get used to seeing violence, and you become more tolerant of it."[4]
>
> —Gamer Eric Falascino.

But some individuals lack the ability to control their violent urges, and this is what causes concerns over the connection between game violence and real-life violence. Indeed, there have been cases where the perpetrator of a mass shooting is later discovered to have spent hours playing violent video games. For example, after thirty-four-year-old Aaron Alexis killed thirteen people in a mass shooting at the Washington Navy Yard in September 2013, investigators discovered that he had played violent video games, including *Call of Duty*, for up to sixteen hours at a time. Some of his friends say they suspect Alexis's gaming caused him to become violent.

Nonetheless, experts disagree on whether there is a cause-and-effect relationship between violent games and violent crimes. They also disagree over whether a similar relationship between violent games and antisocial behavior exists. There is an additional divide among those who believe in a link between virtual-world violence and real-world violence. Some contend that only individuals with a preexisting mental illness are at risk of being negatively affected by playing violent games, but others argue that even those without mental illness might be at risk. In an attempt to resolve such disagreements, studies into possible connections between violent video games and violent crimes are ongoing.

Video Games and Mass Shootings

The Advanced Law Enforcement Rapid Response Training (AL-ERRT) Center at Texas State University defines mass shootings as instances when a gunman opens fire in a public place specifically to commit mass murder, with at least one of the targets being someone unknown to the gunman. These are not shootings motivated by gang violence, nor are they accidental or incidental shootings that take place during the commission of some other crime. Still, they have been growing more common in the United States.

Statistics on Shootings

According to a study conducted by ALERRT for the FBI that was released in January 2014, the annual number of mass shootings in the United States has tripled since 2008. There were five mass shootings per year in America from 2000 through 2008 compared to sixteen per year from 2009 through 2012. In 2013 there were fifteen mass shootings.

In examining the mass shootings that occurred from 2009 through 2012, ALERRT found that 49 percent took place at businesses—retail stores, office buildings, factories, and warehouses—and 29 percent at schools. The remainder occurred at other public places, including a military base, a church, and a theater. However, in 18 percent of the cases the shooter started the attack in one place and finished it at another. In 55 percent of the cases the shooter had some kind of connection with the location of the shooting.

In addition, all of the mass shootings that took place from 2000 to 2012 involved a single shooter, 94 percent of whom were male. The youngest shooter during this period was thirteen years old, and the oldest was eighty-eight. These individuals shot an average of five people during their attacks and killed an average of two. Fifty-nine percent carried a handgun and 26 percent a rifle, although one-third of the shooters brought multiple weapons. Five percent wore body armor.

The ALERRT study did not provide statistics regarding the popularity of violent video games among mass shooters. However, when a mass shooting occurs, further investigation often reveals that the perpetrator played violent video games. This is not unusual given the popularity of such games. But in many cases the circumstances surrounding the crime lead people to question whether a violent game inspired the mass shooting.

A *Call of Duty* Connection

One of the most prominent examples of this involves twenty-four-year-old Tristan van der Vlis, who committed a mass shooting in the town of Alphen aan den Rijn, Netherlands. On April 9, 2011, dressed in camouflage pants and a bomber jacket, he went to the busy Ridderhof mall with a semiautomatic rifle, a .45-caliber pistol, and a .44 Magnum revolver. He fired more than a hundred bullets into the crowd, killing six people and wounding seventeen before killing himself. His victims included children and the elderly.

Van der Vlis had a history of psychiatric problems and had tried to commit suicide at least twice before his death. A member of a shooting club, he was also enamored with guns and managed to purchase the semiautomatic rifle despite the fact that the possession of such weapons is illegal in the Netherlands. But the media focused on the fact that before the massacre van der Vlis had spent hours playing the game *Call of Duty: Modern Warfare 2*.

Reporters noted that one component of this game, a mission commonly known as the Airport Massacre, has features that are similar to van der Vlis's crime. The goal of this mission (which is the fourth level of the game) is for the player, in the role of an undercover CIA agent trying to infiltrate a terrorist group, to participate in the group's attack on innocent civilians in an airport terminal. While pretending to be a terrorist the player does not need to kill any civilians; however, no penalties are incurred for doing so, and many players feel the situation demands it. Van der Vlis was among those who chose to participate in the game massacre; in this scenario, the layout of the game's terminal is remarkably similar to the mall where he commit-

A woman lays flowers at a memorial to the victims of a 2011 mass shooting in the Netherlands. The shooter's murderous actions may have been fueled by his passion for violent video games.

ted his real-life killings. His movements at the mall were also similar to those he would have made within the game environment, and he performed certain actions in the same order as they might occur in the game. Another similarity is that the shooter dies at the end of the game level, although he is killed by the terrorists rather than by his own hand.

Novelist Emile van Veen, who has written a thriller in which terrorists use computer games to rehearse their attacks, suggests that van der Vlis used *Modern Warfare 2* as a way to practice how he was going to carry out his mass shooting. Others say that the idea for the shooting came while van der Vlis was playing the airport terminal level of the game. In either case, many people believe that his actions at the mall show that his game play influenced his choices during the shooting.

Choosing Weaponry

There has also been at least one instance in which a violent video game appears to have influenced a mass shooter's choice of weaponry. The shooter was thirty-two-year-old Anders Behring Breivik. On July 22, 2011, Breivik fired at teens attending a political summer camp on an island approximately 25 miles (40 km) from Oslo, Norway. For roughly an hour and a half, Breivik shot people as they ran, including those who dived into the water to escape him, and returned to some of the wounded to finish them off. He killed sixty-nine people and injured sixty-six before surrendering to police.

Because Breivik left writings to explain his actions, investigators into the massacre were able to determine that his motivations were tied to his political beliefs. However, his testimony during his trial for the murders suggested a video game connection as well. As with van der Vlis, Breivik had spent many hours playing the video game *Call of Duty: Modern Warfare 2*, and he testified that the game gave him the idea to equip his weapon with a holographic sight because this is what the game's first-person shooters use. In fact, he said that had it not been for the holographic sight, he might not have been able to kill so many people. Breivik explained,

> If you are familiar with a holographic sight, it's built up in such a way that you could have given it to your grandmother and she would have been a super marksman. It's designed to be used by anyone. In reality it requires very little training to use it in an optimal way. But of course it does help if you've practiced using a simulator [like *Modern Warfare 2*].[5]

Transferrable Skills?

Breivik also testified that the skills acquired from playing a first-person shooter game can translate into real-world skills because such a game "consists of many hundreds of different tasks [involved with killing people] and some of these tasks can be compared with an attack, for real."[6] In addition, Breivik said that *Modern Warfare 2* affected his decisions and actions preceding and during the attack. In a diary entry

A Shooter Blames His Gaming

Sometime before 9:55 p.m. on **March 8, 2013**, fourteen-year-old Nathon Brooks pried open his parents' gun safe to obtain a .22-caliber pistol, then went to their bedroom and shot them while they slept, hitting his father in the back of the head and his mother in the face and hand. Though both of them were seriously injured, Brooks's father managed to call 911. Nathon Brooks told the arriving officers that an intruder had committed the shooting, but later, after the truth came out, he blamed video games for the crime. Specifically, Brooks said that he had recently been trying to quit playing violent video games because they were making him violent—although he admitted that he started having thoughts of murdering his parents when he was only eight years old. He also said that he had heard voices in his head urging him to kill his parents, and the police determined that Brooks had a history of troubled behavior suggesting that he had a mental illness. However, the reason the shooting took place when it did was because Brooks's parents had just grounded him from using his electronic devices, including those he was using to play video games, as punishment for stealing his father's credit card. He is currently awaiting trial on charges of two counts of first-degree attempted murder.

from February 2010, he called the game "the best military simulator out there," adding, "I see [*Modern Warfare 2*] more as a part of my training-simulation than anything else. . . . You can more or less completely simulate actual operations."[7]

Other entries show that Breivik was thinking of his plans for the massacre in gaming terms. Tom Law, a freelance writer who provides dialogue for video games, noted after studying the entries, "His writing often feels more like an instruction manual for a game than a terrorist manifesto. There are rules to learn, ranks to 'level-up' through, scenarios to complete and medals to unlock."[8]

Some gaming experts disagree with the notion that someone could learn real-life military skills simply from playing a game. For example, Paul Tassi, who writes about video games, technology, and the Internet for *Forbes* magazine, says that "being good at *Call of Duty* makes you about as competent a soldier as playing Dr. Mario makes you a cardiovascular surgeon."[9] However, Dave Grossman, a retired lieutenant colonel in the US Army, argues that there is ample proof that gaming skills translate into real-world skills.

As an example, he cites the case of a fourteen-year-old mass shooter in Paducah, Kentucky, who, although he had no prior shooting experience, fired at eight schoolmates and was able to hit all of them, five in the head and three in the upper torso. Grossman says, "I train numerous elite military and law enforcement organizations around the world. When I tell them of this achievement they are stunned. Nowhere in the annals of military or law enforcement history can we find an equivalent 'achievement.'"[10]

> "Where does a 14-year-old boy who never fired a gun before get the skill and the will to kill? Video games and media violence."[13]
>
> —Dave Grossman, a retired lieutenant colonel in the US Army.

Indeed, the US military and law enforcement agencies use video games as a way to improve people's shooting skills, and studies have shown that practicing with virtual guns can improve even a civilian's accuracy with real guns. In one recent study conducted at Ohio State University, just twenty minutes of playing a first-person shooter game made college students more accurate when shooting at a mannequin. It also made study participants much more likely to fire at the mannequin's head than at the torso. The coauthor of the study, Brad Bushman, concludes, "For good and bad, video game players are learning lessons that can be applied in the real world."[11]

Bushman stresses that he is not saying such games encourage people to commit real-life acts of violence. It was not his study's purpose to determine whether such a cause-and-effect relationship exists. "But," he says, "this study suggests these games can teach people to shoot more accurately and aim to the head." Therefore, he adds, "we shouldn't be too quick to dismiss violent video games as just harmless fun in a fantasy world."[12]

"The Will to Kill"

Grossman suggests that violent video games can provide players not only with the necessary skills to commit a mass shooting but also the motivation to fire into a crowd of innocent people. In regard to the

Kentucky killer, he says, "Where does a 14-year-old boy who never fired a gun before get the skill and the will to kill? Video games and media violence."[13]

Grossman argues that this "will to kill" arises primarily from two aspects of gaming. First, he believes, playing violent video games desensitizes players to violence, hardening their emotions to the point where they can kill in real life. Second, he argues that children are being conditioned to engage in violent acts by being rewarded during game play for every violent act they commit. As a result, he says, "Our kids are learning to kill and learning to like it."[14] He also says that this conditioning can affect their actions in the real world: "By sitting and mindlessly killing countless thousands of fellow members of your own species without any ramification or repercussions, we are teaching skills and concepts and values that transfer immediately anytime they get a real weapon in their hand."[15]

Grossman compares this kind of conditioning to what occurred in the US military after World War II. In his book *On Killing*, he re-

United States Marines practice their aim at a firing range. Soldiers often train using targets with human silhouettes to desensitize them to killing other human beings. Many believe the first-person shooter aspect of many video games encourages the same desensitization.

ports that many US soldiers who had participated in the war later admitted that they sometimes only pretended to fire their weapons or took longer than necessary to reload them because of their reluctance to kill fellow human beings. So the US military changed the way it trained people to kill. Specifically, it had soldiers fire at targets that were the silhouettes of men rather than the traditional bull's-eye, and it rewarded accurate marksmanship and fast shooting with medals and other incentives. In this way, soldiers were conditioned to see the image of a man and shoot without thinking. As a result, Grossman says, 90 percent of US combatants in the next major war involving the United States, the Vietnam War (1956–1975), reported being able to fire at enemies without hesitation.

Given this result, some people argue that playing violent video games makes gamers more capable of killing real human beings and of shooting first without thinking. They also argue that playing shooting games, whether from a first-person or third-person perspective, can lead certain gamers to believe that some human beings are more deserving of being shot than others. According to Jack Thompson, an antigaming activist who has brought lawsuits against the makers of violent games, if someone spends hours playing a game in which police officers are killed, that person learns that police officers are valid targets.

Lack of Study Controls

However, Christopher J. Ferguson, a psychology professor at Stetson University in DeLand, Florida, who has studied the effects of playing violent games, says that people who express such views are merely providing an opinion, not a fact based on valid data. He specifically criticizes Bushman for citing flawed studies to support his views. (The US Supreme Court deemed them flawed while deciding in 2011 to strike down a ban on selling violent video games to minors.) Ferguson explains that these studies failed to control for important variables, such as a family history of violence and/or whether the player lived in a violent environment, and he reports that studies with better methodology have found either no link or a weak link between video game violence and real-life violence.

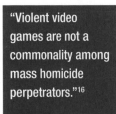

"Violent video games are not a commonality among mass homicide perpetrators."[16]

—*Psychology professor Christopher J. Ferguson.*

Ferguson agrees that there is no such link, and he criticizes Bushman for suggesting that violent video games play a part in mass shootings: "Contrary to Dr. Bushman's suggestion, violent video games are not a commonality among mass homicide perpetrators. The impression that a link exists is a classic illusory correlation in which society notes the cases that fit and ignores those that don't."[16]

As examples of ignored cases, Ferguson cites three mass shootings involving an older gunman who had no experience playing violent video games: seventy-year-old Arthur Douglas Harmon, sixty-two-year-old William Spengler, and sixty-five-year-old Jimmy Lee Dykes. Ferguson contends that "since these incidents don't fit the common social narrative of the mad gamer, they are simply ignored."[17] In other words, Ferguson believes that the media fails to pay attention to these shootings because they show that nongamers are just as capable of committing mass shootings as gamers.

Different Circumstances

However, the circumstances of the killings committed by the men Ferguson mentions are different from those involving gamers. Perpetrators with gaming experience often seek out and target innocent victims in much the same way as occurs in a first-person shooter game, which is why some people suspect a cause-and-effect relationship between violent gaming and mass shootings. But Ferguson's cases do not involve the kind of dispassionate targeting that might remind someone of a first-person shooter game.

Specifically, Harmon's attack, which killed one and wounded two, arose out of an emotional dispute at a mediation meeting related to a lawsuit. Spengler's seems to have been triggered by problems in a relationship as well; he killed his sister in the home they shared, then set fire to the house and shot at responding firefighters, killing two and wounding two. Dykes killed a school bus driver in order to take a five-year-old boy hostage, then fired at but failed to kill law enforcement officers who responded to the hostage situation.

Assessing Blame

But even when a mass shooting has features similar to those of a first-person shooter game, many people say it is wrong to blame video gaming for such crimes. Research has yet to find incontrovertible evidence that such blame would be warranted. Yet in the aftermath of a mass shooting involving a gamer, the media's reaction suggests that such evidence does exist. Matt Peckham of *Time* magazine complained about this after Breivik's attack, saying that it was the result of "news networks that understand perfectly well the hunger for cause-and-effect explanations, or barring that, a flat-out scapegoat."[18]

Peckham notes that people often create scapegoats when they are looking for straightforward explanations that might not exist. In choosing scapegoats, he explains, they often turn to things that are unfamiliar and therefore untrustworthy:

When horrible things happen, we look for simple answers, for easy rationalizations—ways to essentially say, Oh, *this* is why so-and-so did such-and-such. We want the "why" right now, when the spotlight's on. We want the dots connected, and we want them to correspond with our suspicions about new, ultra-popular activities, like dancing to jazz music in the 1920s, or reading comics in the 1950s, or listening to rock 'n' roll in the 1960s, or playing *Dungeons & Dragons* in the 1980s—or playing violent video games pretty much from the 1990s on.[19]

Games Versus Guns

Others argue that it is just as inaccurate to blame video games for mass shootings as it would be to blame guns. Paul Tassi holds this view:

> [If, before the attack, the gunman] went to a gun range every single day for the past year, a place that *actually* trains you how to hit person-shaped targets with a real gun firing real bullets in your hands, would we be talking about how shooting ranges are to blame? Would we want them all closed down for fear someone else might learn how to shoot a gun and kill someone?[20]

However, a 2013 Public Policy poll found that 67 percent of Americans belonging to the Republican Party, which opposes gun control, believe that video games are a bigger safety threat than guns. Only 14 percent believe that guns are a bigger threat than video games. The National Rifle Association (NRA) has also blamed video games for mass shootings.

In December 2012, at a press conference following a mass shooting at a Connecticut elementary school that resulted in the deaths of twenty-six people, most of them children, NRA executive vice president Wayne LaPierre said, "There exists in this country, sadly, a callous, corrupt and corrupting shadow industry that sells and stows

National Rifle Association (NRA) executive vice president Wayne LaPierre blames video games such as Kindergarten Killers *(projected on the video screen) for encouraging real-life violence.*

violence against its own people. Here's one, it's called 'Kindergarten Killers.'"[21] LaPierre was referring to a free online first-person shooter game in which players take the role of an elementary school janitor who kills a teacher and then proceeds to shoot at children throughout the school grounds.

Many experts on violent crime have criticized LaPierre's comments. For example, Ferguson complains that "the NRA is arguing that the problem is imaginary guns, not real guns."[22] Other experts responded to the NRA comments by citing data from the largest world markets for video games. In these countries, crime statistics do not appear to bear out the theory that video games are tied to gun violence. As Max Fisher of the *Washington Post* says,

It's true that Americans spend billions of dollars on video games every year and that the United States has the highest firearm murder rate in the developed world. But other countries where video games are popular have much lower firearm-related murder rates. In fact, countries where video game consumption is highest tend to be some of the safest countries in the world, likely a product of the fact that developed or rich countries, where consumers can afford expensive games, have on average much less violent crime.

Fisher adds that "this data actually suggests a slight *downward* shift in violence as video game consumption increases."[23]

Cause and Effect

Many of the most popular video games do contain a great deal of violence. But it is difficult to establish a true cause-and-effect relationship between playing those games and perpetrating mass murder. Virginia psychologist Stanton Samenow, who has studied the psychological effects of video gaming, says that although "the argument can be made that in terms of taste and public opinion, there is too much gratuitous violence in video games . . . millions of people play violent video games and the overwhelming number wouldn't dream of enacting what they see on the screen."[24] Efforts to understand what role, if any, video games play in such crimes are likely to continue.

> "Millions of people play violent video games and the overwhelming number wouldn't dream of enacting what they see on the screen."[24]
>
> —Virginia psychologist Stanton Samenow.

Antisocial Behavior

In trying to determine whether there is a connection between playing violent video games and committing violent crimes, researchers have looked at a variety of antisocial behaviors displayed by gamers. Acts of aggression or violence have been their primary focus. However, sexism, racism, and views related to morality and ethics have been studied as well. Such studies are typically conducted by having people play violent video games and then examining how gaming might have affected their attitudes and behavior.

Researching Aggression

In January 2014, researchers from the University of Innsbruck, Austria, released the results of a meta-analytic review of ninety-eight independent studies with a combined total of 36,965 test subjects into how playing violent video games influences behavior. (A meta-analysis studies a large amount of data to look for overall trends.) Researchers concluded that there was a significant link between violent video gaming and social outcomes. In fact, the researchers reported unequivocally that "violent video games increase aggression and aggression-related variables and decrease prosocial outcomes."[25]

In commenting on this analysis, Jean M. Twenge, an associate professor of psychology at San Diego State University, notes that it included only studies that had sound methodology. Specifically, these studies had test subjects play either a violent or a nonviolent game but randomly assigned which game each subject played. This is important, Twenge says, to ensure that those playing the violent games are not all aggressive people who are naturally drawn to such games.

Because Twenge trusts the results of this meta-analysis, which found that playing violent video games doubled or tripled the number of players who were highly aggressive after a gaming session, she is dismayed that it has not caused more concern among the public:

> If a large meta-analysis found that kids who eat candy were more likely to hit other kids—with a doubling or tripling in the number who hit really hard—few people would have a problem saying kids shouldn't eat candy. Yet because many people enjoy playing video games, they are reluctant to take action to keep people from playing these games—even if it leads to aggression or violence.[26]

Twenge acknowledges that crime statistics show that violent crime has gone down even as video games have become more violent. Yet she argues that this reduction in crime could be the result of many other factors, including changing demographics (because senior citizens, for example, are less likely to commit violent crimes than young men) and improvements in law enforcement practices. She also says that she has no illusion that eliminating violent video games will end mass shootings. However, Twenge firmly believes that eliminating them will reduce the amount of aggression in the world.

Gaming Frustrations

But some people question whether the aggression demonstrated in studies of gaming effects is actually caused by the violent video game. Instead, they suggest that the aggression is due to researchers not giving players enough time to become familiar with the game. They contend that the duration of play is often so short that players leave the game frustrated over being unable to perform well; in acting out this

"If a large meta-analysis found that kids who eat candy were more likely to hit other kids . . . few people would have a problem saying kids shouldn't eat candy. Yet because many people enjoy playing video games, they are reluctant to take action to keep people from playing these games—even if it leads to aggression or violence."[26]

—*Psychologist Jean M. Twenge.*

frustration, they exhibit more aggression than normal. Ferguson explains:

> Since . . . violent games tend to be more difficult to learn and have more complex controls than non-violent games, it appears that many participants in these experiments may simply have been frustrated by being cut off so quickly before they even learned how to play, rather than by the violent content of the game. Letting them play long enough to learn the game, or simply providing violent and non-violent games of equal complexity, erases the effects.[27]

Indeed, researchers at the University of Rochester in New York released a study in April 2014 that found that it was frustration with game play rather than violent content that caused players to become more aggressive. The six hundred study participants played both violent and nonviolent games, after which they were tested for aggressive behavior. There were various ways this behavior was tested, but in one the test subject was given the power to decide how long a fellow gamer would have to keep his or her hand in freezing cold water. Those who had just played a difficult game that caused them to struggle assigned far longer times than those who had an easy time playing their game. Lead researcher Andrew Przybylski reports that it did not matter whether the game was violent or nonviolent. Instead, he says, "When people feel they have no control over the outcome of the game, that leads to aggression."[28]

> "When people feel they have no control over the outcome of the game, that leads to aggression."[28]
>
> —Gaming violence researcher Andrew Przybylski.

Sexualized Content

Other studies, however, seem to show that game content does affect behavior. For example, studies into the effects of gaming on attitudes toward women suggest that playing certain types of video games can change the way women think and/or act because of the way characters of their gender are portrayed in these games. Specifically, in first-person

An advertisement for the game Grand Theft Auto *displays the over-sexualized female figures often depicted in such games. Some psychologists argue that female gamers can subconsciously take in such depictions, leading to poor self-esteem.*

games for mature audiences, female characters are far more likely to be portrayed in sexualized ways than male characters. This creates issues because of how gamers relate to virtual characters—particularly a character being used as the gamer's avatar, or stand-in.

Jesse Fox, Jeremy N. Bailenson, and Liz Tricase of Stanford University's Department of Communications, who conducted a study into the effect of the sexualization of gaming characters, explain that a unique relationship is forged during game play between virtual humans and the real humans they represent:

> Unlike images in other media, virtual humans are typically designed to be engaging and to respond to a user's actions. This dynamic creates a new and powerful experience beyond passive media consumption; . . . users often react to virtual humans in natural and social ways. Also, rather than merely observing characters, users may . . . experience the virtual

body as their own, which has been shown to have stronger effects than passively watching them. Because of the enhanced realism, the opportunities for interactivity, and the experience of embodiment, it is possible that these representations will have powerful effects on users' beliefs, attitudes, and behaviors offline as well.[29]

According to the researchers, female gamers who play violent games in which women are seen not as individuals but as sex objects can gradually internalize the messages of the game: that women really are objects and are valued only if their appearance matches what society deems ideal. As a result, they can experience eating disorders, a preoccupation with their bodies, and depression. In addition, the researchers believe that playing violent games in which female characters are objectified and sexually mistreated by male characters can cause gamers to be more accepting of violence against women in the real world and more callous in regard to the victims of such violence.

Rape Myths

As part of their study into how female gamers internalize game messages about women, the researchers had each test subject wear a head-mounted Oculus Rift–style display (a device that provides a personal viewing experience) that allowed them to see themselves as a character in a video game. Each participant saw her own face atop a virtual body; some of the bodies were sexualized, but others were not. Shortly thereafter each participant was asked questions that determined her attitudes about rape and about how she felt about her own body. The questions were posed in such a way that the women believed they were being asked for purposes of designing a future study on these issues.

The women's answers showed that those whose virtual body was sexualized were far more likely to express an acceptance of rape myths, which are false beliefs about rape that typically put the blame for a rape on the victim. An example of a rape myth is the notion that a woman who dresses provocatively is essentially asking to be raped.

Playing *Grand Theft Auto* for Real

At around 2 a.m. on September 23, 2013, twenty-year-old Zachary Burgess, a student at Auburn University in Alabama, spotted a truck in a parking lot with its engine running and its driver missing. He got behind the wheel, ignoring the protests of a woman sitting in the passenger seat, and began driving around the parking lot. Witnesses watched him slam into nine other cars, then jump out of the truck and run away. They chased him down and held him until police arrived. Burgess told them that he had taken the truck and smashed into the cars because he wanted to see what it would be like to play the video game *Grand Theft Auto* for real. He was charged with stealing the truck, kidnapping the woman, and committing nine counts of hit-and-run for damaging the vehicles he struck.

This was a matter of concern to the researchers because studies have shown that women who have internalized rape myths are less likely to take precautions against being raped. For example, if they are not dressed provocatively then they might feel they are immune to a sexual attack. The researchers also note, in regard to the possibility that men might be experiencing the same effect, that men who have internalized rape myths are more likely to rape.

In another study, Fox eliminated the headsets and had participants play as a sexualized avatar in a desktop computer game called *Second Life*. She found that test subjects engaged in self-objectification (seeing themselves as objects) and accepted rape myths to roughly the same degree as in the headset study. After discussing this study with Fox, Joseph Bernstein, who writes on gaming issues for the website BuzzFeed, reported,

> Beyond the obvious nefarious effect of internalizing rape-culture myths, this kind of self-objectification may produce even more problems for women gamers. Fox pointed out research that has shown that women who are sensitized to their body by a media stimulus have short-term cognitive

impairments. Imagine a situation, then, in which a girl gamer plays as a sexualized avatar, and then performs worse on a school test than she would have otherwise.[30]

Racism

An Ohio State University study released in March 2014 suggests that violent video games can also promote racism, particularly in the form of negative stereotypes against blacks. For this study white college students were divided into two groups: one group was 60 percent male, and the other was 65 percent female. Participants were randomly assigned to play a video game as either a black character or a white one. The characters were identical in body type, but the white avatar had a conservative haircut and the black one cornrows. In addition, the black character spoke with an inner-city dialect.

> "Imagine a situation, then, in which a girl gamer plays as a sexualized avatar, and then performs worse on a school test than she would have otherwise."[30]
>
> —Joseph Bernstein, who writes on gaming issues for the website BuzzFeed.

For the first part of the study, members of the first group played a third-person game, *Saints Row 2*, in which they performed one of two missions. One mission was violent (a prison break), and the other was nonviolent (merely finding a church). Afterward they were asked to agree or disagree with various statements about black people, then shown photos of black people and asked to match words such as *joy* or *evil* with each one. For the second part of the study, members of the second group played one of two violent fighting games: *Fight Night Round 4* or *WWE Smackdown vs. Raw 2010*. Participants then were asked to match pictures of white or black faces with various ordinary objects, some of them weapons. Members of both groups were also asked to determine how much hot sauce another player—whom they did not see and who did not actually exist—would have to eat.

The hot sauce test is one of many variations on a standard way of measuring aggression—that is, by seeing how much punishment one person is willing to inflict on another. In this case it suggested that test subjects who had played a violent game as a black character were significantly more aggressive afterward than those who played the same game as a white character. Specifically, those who had been exposed to game violence doled out 115 percent more hot sauce.

The other tests revealed similar differences. Participants who played violent games as black characters were more likely to use negative words in responding to photos of blacks, agree with racist statements, and associate blacks with weapons than those who played as white characters. Consequently, Brad Bushman, one of the authors of the study, concludes that "playing a violent video game as a black character reinforces harmful stereotypes that blacks are violent."[31]

Bushman notes that this runs contrary to what many people expect. He says, "Usually, taking the perspective of a minority person is seen as a good thing, as a way to evoke empathy." Indeed, a 2014 study led by researchers at the University of Barcelona, Spain, found that experiencing virtual reality—via a virtual-reality headset and body-tracking suit—as a black avatar reduced racism in lighter skinned study participants. But this study did not involve any gaming; participants simply inhabited a virtual body and were able to see themselves reflected in a virtual mirror while doing so. Bushman suggests, therefore, that it is the game play that encourages players to become racist "because being a black character in a video game is almost synonymous with being a violent character."[32]

However, some experts have questioned the conclusions of Bushman's study, largely because the study relies on the implicit association test (IAT). A popular way to measure attitudes, the IAT asks test subjects to associate images or things with positive or negative words. The more quickly and easily a test subject makes the association, the stronger the association is believed to be. Conversely, if a test subject takes a long time to provide a positive word, then the test subject is deemed to have an implicit negative view—that is, a view that is thought but not expressed.

Tyler Black, a psychiatrist who has studied the connection between violent video games and real-world violence, calls IAT responses proxies, or stand-ins, that might or might not represent actual attitudes. He similarly suggests that hot sauce punishments might not indicate how aggressive someone will be in a real-world situation. According to Black, "We're not sure of the relationship between IAT and real world racism, stereotypes, etc. It . . . doesn't 'prove negative racial thought.' In the same way, unless homicide/violence by way of hot sauce becomes a common method of assault, it too is a proxy for violence. How does hot sauce selection relate to real world violence?"[33]

Black also criticizes the study on the basis of what researchers call confounding variables, which are things that might be influencing the subject's responses but are not the concern of the study. For

A video game that features rapper 50 Cent is promoted at a trade show. Critics argue that video games almost always depict blacks as violent predators.

example, Black says that because the IATs were conducted after the gaming and not before, we do not know what the test subjects' attitudes toward blacks were to begin with. It is also unknown whether their negative IAT responses were based on the fact that they were playing as someone who was a different color from themselves, regardless of whether that color was black. "If the avatar was green and the IAT about negative green stereotypes," Black says, "would it show an effect?" Similarly, he says, "If the character were forced [to be] female, stereotypically nonviolent, would the IAT of male participants have shifted toward bias of negative attitudes toward females [rather than blacks]? How about other races?"[34]

> "Playing a violent video game as a black character reinforces harmful stereotypes that blacks are violent."[31]
>
> —Brad Bushman, video game researcher.

Black also suggests that the results might have been due to the way the human brain works: "I played *Mass Effect* as a female Commander Shepard. I am confident that this changed my IAT scores for female/aggression or female/weapon immediately after playing. This reflects the brain's desire to make efficient connections, more than it likely does an evolving stereotype of female violence in my brain."[35]

Immoral Behavior

Other researchers believe that playing violent video games can actually change the brain in ways that make people more aggressive. David Walsh, a child psychologist who has studied the relationship between violent video games and physical aggression, says that the brains of young people are particularly vulnerable to such effects. The reason, he says, lies in the way that the brain develops: "The teenage brain is different from the adult brain. The impulse control center of the brain, the part of the brain that enables us to think ahead, consider consequences, manage urges . . . that's under construction during the teenage years. In fact, the wiring of that is not completed until the early 20s."[36] Walsh also says that if a person comes from a troubled background, the impulse control center can be even more compromised after prolonged gaming, which can make the person likely to behave in antisocial ways.

Game-Created Biases

In January 2012, nineteen-year-old Anthony Graziano of New Jersey firebombed the home of a rabbi and several synagogues. Because he had targeted only Jewish people, Graziano was charged not only with nine counts of first-degree attempted murder and one count of aggravated arson but also with one count of bias intimidation. The term *bias intimidation* refers to intimidating people or groups on the basis of race, color, ethnicity, national origin, religion, disability, gender, gender identity or expression, and/or sexual orientation. However, Graziano's attorney, Robert Kalisch, said that Graziano was not to blame for his violence and his biases. Instead, Kalisch said, it was the fault of the video games that Graziano had been playing on his Xbox. Kalisch reported that his client was mentally unstable and insisted that this made him more vulnerable to the effects of exposure to violent gaming, adding, "When you have emotional, psychiatric, psychological problems, and you get involved in these games, the whole aura of it pervades and it's not a game anymore. It becomes reality."

Quoted in Evan Narcisse, "Video Games Blamed for Synagogue Firebombings," Kotaku, January 31, 2012. http://kotaku.com.

A study in Italy led by psychologist Alessandro Gabbiadini yielded similar findings. Specifically, it showed that playing a violent video game for just thirty-five minutes can lead gamers to exhibit a lack of self-control and an increase in aggressive behavior. This aggression was measured in a way similar to the hot sauce test, by allowing participants to decide whether to blast someone else with a loud, unpleasant noise delivered through headphones. The study also suggested that violent gaming can lead to immoral thinking and behavior.

The study involved 172 high school students. Half of the participants played a nonviolent game (*Pinball 3D* or *Mini Golf 3D*), and the other half played a violent one (*Grand Theft Auto III* or *Grand Theft Auto: San Andreas*). To assess morality, the researchers provided all gamers with access to candy and told them they could eat it, but not excessively. Later the researchers measured the candy and found that players of the violent game took far more than players of the nonviolent game. In a similar test, after the gaming the participants were each given an envelope filled with raffle tickets and told to complete ten logic problems, then reward themselves with one raffle ticket for each problem they solved correctly. Later the researchers compared the number of tickets taken from the envelopes with the number of problems solved correctly and discovered that far more of those who had played a violent game took more tickets than they deserved.

In addition, when participants were asked after the gaming whether they agreed or disagreed with various statements related to morals, such as whether it is relatively harmless to shoplift, the answers of those who had played a violent game suggested that they were more accepting of immoral behavior. However, the researchers also discovered that teens who already had difficulties behaving ethically were far more likely than others to be adversely affected by violent video games in regard to morals.

The researchers say that more studies are needed to verify their results. But in reporting on these results, journalist Tom Jacobs says that they already "add important nuance to the debate" regarding whether violent video games cause aggressiveness and other antisocial behavior. In fact, Jacobs finds the research so convincing that he believes that they have shown "violent video games can, and do, impact players' attitudes and behaviors. And not for the better."[37] Others, however, argue that a great deal more research is needed before this can be stated unequivocally.

Video Games and Mental Illness

Chapter Three

The perpetrators of some of the most notorious mass shootings in recent years have been not only players of violent video games but also apparently the mentally ill. This seems to have been the case, for example, with Adam Lanza, who killed twenty children and six adults at Sandy Hook Elementary School in Connecticut on December 14, 2012. Before the massacre he also killed his mother in her own bed. Lanza played violent video games for hours on end and was obsessed with getting high body counts in these games—an obsession that law enforcement officials believe he carried over into his real-life mass shooting.

Shortly after the shooting a veteran police officer told a reporter anonymously that investigators believed Lanza went to the school because "it was the way to pick up the easiest points." Similarly, according to the informant, investigators believed that Lanza killed himself after the shooting as a way to keep his points. As the informant explained, "It's why he didn't want to be killed by law enforcement. In the code of the gamer, even a deranged gamer like this [one], if somebody else kills you, they get your points."[38]

No Indication of Violence

Lanza had multiple mental problems. According to a report released in January 2014, in 2006 Lanza's father arranged for him to have a three-hour psychiatric evaluation by experts at Yale University's Child Study Center. They diagnosed Lanza with severe autism, isolationist and antisocial tendencies, depression, and obsessive-compulsive disorder (OCD) and referred him to a psychiatric nurse on staff at the center, Kathleen Koenig, for therapy. After further examination, she strongly recommended that Lanza take medication for his depression and OCD. However, his mother rejected this recommendation and soon stopped bringing him to Koenig.

Later Koenig told police that during her sessions with Lanza he had asked her about other mental conditions, most notably schizophrenia and psychosis, framing his questions as though he were asking out of general curiosity rather than in relation to his own problems. This suggests that he might have been worried he had these conditions, both of which can sometimes lead to violent behavior. However, Koenig reports that there were no indications that Lanza was violent—and because he did not seem to be a danger to himself or others, she could not force him to continue treatment.

Harold Schwartz, a psychiatrist who participated in a Connecticut commission that studied the Lanza shooting, says the fact that Koenig did not believe Lanza to be violent is not surprising. As he explains, "The research is pretty clear that mentally ill individuals as a class are not significantly more violent than individuals without mental illness. Regarding extremely serious acts of violence, only a small proportion is committed by people with severe mental illnesses."[39]

People light candles for victims of the 2012 mass shooting at Sandy Hook Elementary School. Shooter Adam Lanza was an obsessive video gamer and was also mentally ill—a combination that some psychologists believe can lead to a mass shooting.

Reducing Violence?

Some studies suggest that playing violent video games can actually reduce people's real-life hostility by giving them an outlet for their aggression. In one such study reported in 2011, researchers Michael R. Ward, an economist at the University of Texas in Arlington, A. Scott Cunningham of Baylor University, and Benjamin Engelstätter of the Center for European Economic Research in Mannheim, Germany, examined week-to-week sales figures for violent video games in various locations and compared them to the number of violent crimes that occurred in those locations after a heavy sales period. They found that more sales meant less crime. Presuming that people who have received a new video game play that game for many hours, this suggests that heavy game play reduces rather than increases real-life violent tendencies. However, it might also mean that gamers are so busy playing their new games that they have no inclination to leave their gaming devices in order to commit a violent crime.

However, experts say that people whose mental illnesses are untreated are at more risk of committing a violent act than ones who are receiving care for their illness. Bandy Lee, a researcher at the Yale School of Medicine who specializes in psychiatric violence, reports, "When mental illness is well-treated in society, patients are not necessarily more violent. But when they go untreated and they are allowed to become severely ill, then we're seeing a larger share of violence being committed by mentally-ill individuals."[40] This suggests that when a mentally ill person commits a violent crime, the media should be more concerned with whether that person has received treatment for his or her illness than with whether that person played violent video games.

Worsening Symptoms

However, some experts believe that playing violent video games excessively can worsen mental health. Developmental psychologist Douglas Gentile of Iowa State University, for example, has conducted studies indicating there is a correlation between heavy gaming and depression in young people. According to Gentile, "The depression seemed to follow the gaming. As kids became addicted—if you want to use that word—then their depression seemed to get worse. And, as they stopped being addicted, the depression seemed to lift."[41]

Gentile also believes that heavy gaming can fuel other mental problems because of how interconnected these problems can be. He explains that "when a person gets one disorder, they often get more. If you've been diagnosed with bipolar disorder, a year or two later you might end up with anxiety problems or social phobias. They all start interacting with each other and make each other worse."[42]

The notion that violent games could worsen mental illnesses, especially those that cause sufferers to confuse fantasy with reality, is a matter of great concern. Current research does not indicate that game play can contribute to the development of psychosis or other serious mental disorders that might lead to violence. Nonetheless, some experts recommend that people with a mental illness, even a relatively minor one, not be exposed to violent gaming. At the very least, they say, such gaming can increase stimulation and adrenaline production. This can unduly agitate the player, possibly disrupting sleep and adversely affecting mood.

A Lack of Empathy

Some people believe that playing violent video games can also reduce empathy, the ability to understand and share the feelings of another person. A lack of empathy can make it easier for people to commit acts of violence against others, and some experts suggest that violent video games encourage this by depersonalizing their victims. For example, if a game involves terrorizing innocent people who live in a poor neighborhood, then this could encourage a lack of empathy toward real-life inhabitants of such neighborhoods.

Experts in human behavior disagree on whether a video game can cause a lack of empathy. In fact, since a lack of empathy is often a warning sign that a serious mental illness is present, some psychologists doubt that any video game could cause this degree of psychological harm. Therefore, some experts say that if a gamer exhibits a lack of empathy, this means that it existed before the gaming, and the gaming is only bringing attention to an existing illness. Henry Jenkins of the Massachusetts Institute of Technology, who supports this position, says, "Media reformers argue that playing violent video games can cause a lack of empathy for real-world victims. Yet, a child who responds to a video game the same way he or she responds to a real-world tragedy could be showing symptoms of being severely emotionally disturbed."[43]

Gamers also note that empathy is a big part of games that put players "in the skin" of a first-person shooter, who might be either a hero or a bad guy. Therefore, as game designer Ken Levine says, "Empathy for the characters is something first person shooters need."[44] Some games can also model empathy for players by featuring characters who show concern for one another. For example, game expert Michael Abbott says that the character of Alyx Vance in the first-person shooter game *Half-Life 2* demonstrates empathy to such a degree that "if you want

A teenager plays a first-person shooter game. A typical gamer will shoot to kill thousands of times and may reduce empathy for others and blur the lines between real-life violence and fantasy, critics argue.

to know what empathy in video games looks like, you need go no further than her."[45]

Manic Episodes

Experts also disagree on whether playing video games can adversely affect someone with bipolar disorder (formerly called manic-depressive disorder). However, people with this disorder have reported that excessive gaming can bring on manic episodes, which might involve extreme elation, high energy, irritability, and impulsivity. In speaking of his own experience with mania and gaming, Dennis Scimeca says, "I experienced severe manic episodes and there was no doubt the game I'd been playing was responsible." But he adds, "It had nothing to do with first person shooters, the specific genre of video game that everyone worries about in the wake of a school shooting." Instead, the games that caused him problems were role-playing games, which he says "exacerbated my bipolar disorder or drew upon unhealthy aspects of my psychology."[46] He suspects this was because his mania, for which he is now receiving treatment, usually involved delusions of grandeur, and playing a game as a character who was better than others allowed him to feed his ego.

Scimeca also reports a more troublesome gaming experience: "The only time I've ever felt like a video game truly tapped into something dark and disturbing in my psyche was when I played *Fallout 3* as a character I named Vault Boy. He was a psychopathic, cruel killer who, to the tune of my boisterous laughter, would slaughter entire towns." Scimeca found his own laughter disturbing but believes it was an expression of repressed anger and insists, "I'm mentally ill, I've gorged on violent video games my entire life, and they've never made me feel like doing harm to another human being." He explains that for him, violent gaming had a positive effect:

> I've *never* taken the ultra-violent, gore-ridden images from Vault Boy's exploits and used them as fodder for fantasies about the real world, because it's not about that. Vault Boy is a conduit into very old anger from before my illness was treated, and by indulging in his exploits I tap into and vomit up all the

accumulated bile. It feels similar to my very early therapy sessions where I was sometimes offered a pillow to punch when I was ranting angrily.[47]

Pathological Gaming

Indeed, some experts believe that video gaming can provide positive outlets for emotions, particularly when used in conjunction with therapy. Studies have shown that playing video games can improve spatial reason and focus, memory formation, strategic planning, muscle control, and fine motor skills as well. However, researchers say that enjoyable game play can also cause the brain to release a pleasure-related chemical called dopamine, and this spike in dopamine can trigger addictive behavior. That is, the pleasure of the spike can cause a corresponding letdown when the dopamine level drops again, and this leads the experiencer to crave more of the activity that caused the spike.

> "I'm mentally ill, I've gorged on violent video games my entire life, and they've never made me feel like doing harm to another human being."[47]
>
> —Gamer Dennis Scimeca, who suffers from bipolar disorder.

For most people, this craving only results in a mild obsession with gaming, one that might lead them occasionally to shirk other, more important tasks but does not interfere with their ability to earn a living or maintain personal relationships. As Gentile reports,

A lot of video gaming isn't the same as an addiction. Some kids can play a lot without having an effect on their lives. It's when you see other areas of your child's life suffer that it may be addiction. Parents might notice that a child doesn't have the same friends any more, or that he's just sitting in his room playing video games all the time. Or, there might be a drop in school performance.[48]

For others, though, excessive gaming is such a serious problem that they feel it is ruining their lives. Experts consider such people to be pathological gamers (a term many prefer over *addicted gamers* because it distinguishes gaming abuse from substance abuse). According to Gentile, roughly 9 percent of Americans can be called pathological gamers, and psychologists who try to help these people say that they can be similar to drug addicts. For example, psychotherapist Hilarie Cash says that most of her clients "have lost jobs, lost marriages, dropped out of college or high school, and their lives have fallen apart. They exhibit all of the standard characteristics [of addiction]. Their behavior is compulsive, they get a high off of it, they do it in spite of negative consequences."[49]

Cash adds that her clients have something else in common with people addicted to a substance: They need more and more of the object of their obsession in order to get the same level of satisfaction from it. As she explains, "People will play . . . an hour of *World of Warcraft*, let's say, but then, after that, it's no longer making them high. They want more. And so they play more. And they develop tolerance over time. . . . Just over a matter of weeks and months, people can end up with a severe addiction."[50]

Addiction-Related Murders

Severe addictive behavior can lead people to commit crimes. Experts say that theft is the most common crime committed by pathological gamers because excessive gaming has caused many to have no other source of income. In some cases, however, this kind of theft can be coupled with a violent crime. For example, in 2011 a fifteen-year-old boy in the province of Nghe An in Vietnam beat a seven-year-old neighbor girl in the head with a rock so he could steal her gold earrings and sell them to fund his online gaming addiction. The girl later died of her injuries.

There have also been cases of gaming addicts committing murder simply to facilitate their ability to keep playing a game for hours on end. For example, at 1 a.m. on April 17, 2014, twenty-four-year-old Cody Wygant of Homosassa, Florida, grew annoyed that his sixteen-month-old son would not stop crying while he was trying to play Xbox games. In order to keep gaming uninterrupted, he put his hand over the child's mouth until the boy passed out, then covered him with a blanket in a way that further blocked the child's airway and went back to his Xbox. Later he discovered that his son was dead, and he was charged with third-degree murder, which is an unplanned killing.

Crimes of Neglect

Authorities subsequently charged Wygant with child neglect as well after they found another baby in the house, a three-month-old girl who had been seriously neglected. In particular, she appeared to have flat-head syndrome, a condition whereby an infant's head is flattened in one spot because the child has been left lying in the same position for hours on end.

This was also the case with a two-year-old who was hospitalized in critical condition in Tulsa, Oklahoma, in October 2011 because of neglect. In addition to having flat-head syndrome, the child was severely underweight and weak. Authorities blamed her condition on her parents' addiction to the online social game *Second Life*. While focusing for hours on the game, authorities said, the parents had ignored the baby's cries to be fed. After taking her to the hospital when it looked like she might be dying, the parents returned home to continue gaming. When police came to talk to them about her condition, they barely interrupted their gaming to ask whether their daughter was in fact dead. Fortunately, the toddler survived. The couple was arrested for neglect and abuse. The situation held a measure of irony: within the world of their game, they had been successfully raising a virtual baby.

Preventing Interference

Parents who are negligent enough to ignore their children's needs because of gaming would probably neglect their children even without access to games. In other words, gaming does not necessarily cause them to be neglectful. Still, any kind of behavioral or substance addiction can increase the likelihood that the sufferer will neglect important aspects of his or her life even to the point of serious harm.

Addictions can also cause people to lash out at loved ones who are trying to separate them from the source of their addiction. Sometimes this lashing out can involve murder. Among the most notable of these cases in regard to pathological gaming involves

The Wrongfulness of His Conduct

In May 2014 twenty-six-year-old Nianthony Martinez was sentenced to twenty-five years to life in prison for the 2008 attempted murder of his ex-girlfriend and the woman he believed turned her against him. His decision to plead guilty was based on his desire to avoid an even longer sentence, but originally he had planned to plead not guilty by reason of insanity. Legal experts believe he was going to use video games as at least a partial excuse for his crimes.

Both Martinez and his friend Angel Gamez—who helped Martinez carry out the attempted murder and received a sentence of fifteen years in prison for his involvement—played *World of Warcraft* together. Gamez's attorney said of the case, "It's hard to believe these young men went from online dragons and elves . . . to the tragic shooting of these poor girls." Martinez's attorney blamed the crime on his client's inability to tell right from wrong, saying, "He has significant mental health issues that impaired his ability to appreciate the wrongfulness of his conduct." Martinez's parents reported that their son had no job and spent nearly all of his time playing video games.

Consequently, legal experts suspect that testimony for the defense would have suggested that playing *World of Warcraft* contributed to Martinez's inability to recognize that killing was wrong. But as his prosecutors note, as a spurned and jealous boyfriend, Martinez had a clear motive for murder that was unrelated to gaming.

Quoted in David Ovalle, "As Trial Looms, Details Emerge About Miami-Dade Video Gamer's Murder Plot," *Miami Herald*, January 12, 2014. www.miamiherald.com.

sixteen-year-old Daniel Petric of Wellington, Ohio. Petric's parents had forbidden him to play violent video games; however, after a friend praised the game *Halo 3*, he decided to purchase it on the sly and sneak it into his house. He then played it on his Xbox console whenever he could get away with it and, when he was home sick during a lengthy illness, developed what many would consider an addiction to the game. He would play for up to eighteen hours straight, often forgoing food and sleep in order to do so. He eventually grew so careless about hiding his gaming that his parents caught him at it. They immediately took the game away and locked it in their safe, which also held a handgun.

A week later, on October 20, 2007, Petric used his father's key to the safe to unlock it and retrieve the game. He took the gun as well, then walked up behind his parents in another room and told them to close their eyes because he had a surprise for them. When they complied, he fired at them multiple times, shooting each of them in the head. His mother died; his father survived but has a seriously disfigured jaw.

In 2009 Petric was found guilty of killing his mother and attempting to kill his father; he was sentenced to twenty-three years to life in prison. At the close of the trial, according to Petric's father, presiding judge James Burge said, "If it weren't for violent video games, I would never have known Daniel Petric."[51] Petric's father also told an interviewer that mental health experts who examined his son concluded that the young man's actions could be blamed on three things: depression over his illness, anger over his parents' confiscation of his game, and his gaming addiction.

Feeling Powerful

Experts say that such crimes can also arise from a need to feel powerful. Petric, for example, undoubtedly felt powerless when his game was taken away. His subsequent actions could have been an attempt to regain the power to game. As many gaming experts note, violent video games often provide the feeling of being powerful. As gamer Paul Runge explains, "Video games are appealing because they allow players to become what they are not. For example, outside the *World of Warcraft (WoW)*, a player may feel weak and vulnerable. However, inside *WoW*, the player is some buff, kickass ogre. A dweebie pantheon of strength."[52]

Former gamer Ryan van Cleave, who wrote an autobiography entitled *Unplugged* to reveal his struggles with his *World of Warcraft* addiction, reports that his pathological behavior was driven largely by the need to feel more powerful. In his book he explains that "playing WoW makes me feel godlike. I have ultimate control and can do what I want with few real repercussions. The real world makes me feel im-

A gamer dresses up as one of the characters in the video game World of Warcraft: Cataclysm at a premiere for the game. The role-playing aspect of such games is appealing to gamers, who may not feel very powerful in their own lives.

potent . . . a computer malfunction, a sobbing child, a suddenly dead cellphone battery—the littlest hitch in daily living feels profoundly disempowering."[53]

Some mental health professionals suggest that playing violent video games can cause someone to become addicted to feeling god-like and that this addiction might result in a desire to experience the same feeling in real life. Such a desire, they say, might be a part of what motivates some gamers to commit mass shootings. This was one of the speculations regarding the first school shooters whose actions the media tried to tie to video gaming. On April 20, 1999, eighteen-year-old Eric Harris and seventeen-year-old Dylan Klebold killed twelve classmates and a teacher at Columbine High School in Colorado before killing themselves. The two young men were fans of two of the earliest first-person shooter games, *Doom* and *Duke Nukem*, and Harris chose the shotgun he used in the massacre based on its similarity to his weapon in *Doom*. Harris and Klebold were also both bullied and were bullies themselves. They had been victimized at school since at least the tenth grade, and by the twelfth grade they were victimizing younger, weaker students, perhaps as a way to reclaim feelings of power.

However, both youths also had psychological problems that preceded their playing of first-person shooter games. Harris had been under the care of a psychiatrist who had put him on a powerful antidepressant. According to psychologist Peter Langman, the author of the book *Why Kids Kill: Inside the Minds of School Shooters*, "These are not ordinary kids who were bullied into retaliation. These are not ordinary kids who played too many video games. These are not ordinary kids who just wanted to be famous. These are simply *not ordinary kids*. These are kids with serious psychological problems."[54]

> "These are not ordinary kids who played too many video games. . . . These are simply *not ordinary kids*. These are kids with serious psychological problems."[54]
>
> —*Psychologist Peter Langman.*

Langman believes that Harris and Klebold were psychopaths, which he describes as people who lack empathy or a conscience, are often narcissistic (egotistically preoccupied with themselves) and sadistic (they enjoy hurting others), and generally do what they want to do without regard for rules, laws, morals, or social conventions. He also reports that young people who commit acts of mass violence fall into one of three categories: psychopaths, psychotics—individuals who suffer from hallucinations, delusions, and/or other symptoms related to their lack of grounding in reality—or people who have been severely traumatized by chronic physical abuse in extremely dysfunctional homes.

These conditions do not arise from playing video games, violent or otherwise. Nor do people without psychoses, experts say, have trouble separating fantasy from reality as a result of their gaming. As Pamela Rutledge, director of the Media Psychology Research Center in Boston notes, for a mentally healthy person

> the realism [of violent video games] heightens the experience and the attention of the player, but that doesn't neces-

sarily mean that it equates in their minds to killing a person. They're already in the context that this is a game, and the fact that the game is realistic heightens the immersion, but that doesn't change the fact that it is a game any more than playing "Battleship" does with little plastic ships.[55]

Experts also note that a psychopath who is also a sadist would typically be drawn to video games that involve hurting and/or killing others, which means that the video gaming is incidental to an underlying mental illness. Many experts say, therefore, that it is wrong to assume that video gaming plays a role in extreme acts of violence.

Legal Responses to Gaming Issues

Every time an act of violence committed by someone who plays violent video games gains widespread media attention, there are calls for bans on violent video games. There are also attempts to restrict the content and/or sale of violent video games. Some of these efforts have been successful initially, only to be later overturned by court decisions.

The *Night Trap* Controversy

The first objections to the violence in gaming were triggered in 1979 by the release of the arcade game *Death Race*, which involved killing gremlins by running over them with a vehicle. The graphics were crude, but parents were appalled that children were being encouraged to kill. Other violent games soon followed, along with more complaints about game content, but it was not until games became more realistic that public officials began to address the issue of violent gaming.

The first of these efforts occurred in December 1993, when then-senator Joe Lieberman began holding Senate subcommittee hearings on violence in gaming. Heavily covered by the media, these hearings provided a platform for politicians to denounce certain games for their violent content. Among the games drawing criticism were the first-person shooter game *Doom*, which would later be associated with the 1999 school shooting at Columbine High School in Colorado, and *Night Trap*, which involved watching virtual rooms in a house via hidden cameras and clicking on an icon whenever a vampiric being known as an Augur appeared on screen.

But whereas *Doom* involved killing people, *Night Trap* involved saving them. Specifically, players who clicked on an icon at the right time would activate a trap, such as a false floor, to capture an Augur, thereby preventing him from killing any of the girls in the house. Players who failed in this task would see a brief video of a bloodless murder or a victim being dragged away by an Augur who was perhaps wielding a blood-draining device, and the death of certain characters would immediately end the game. In other words, any scenes of violence were the result of player error, and to win the game the player had to save people and prevent violence.

Nonetheless, because the politicians involved in the proceedings were largely unfamiliar with their subject matter, they accused *Night Trap* of rewarding violence and called it "disgusting," "shameful," and "ultraviolent."[56] Lieberman even said that players of the game had to try "to trap and kill women."[57] Consequently, most newspaper articles about the hearings reported not on what the game actually consisted of but instead on what the politicians perceived it to be. This resulted in a public outcry against *Night Trap*, and stores began pulling the game from their shelves. Meanwhile, Lieberman aggressively promoted the idea that the federal government should regulate video games.

The Entertainment Software Rating Board

Concerned that this idea would catch fire and ultimately harm their industry, gaming manufacturers addressed the criticism in 1994 by establishing a ratings system for video games similar to the one for motion pictures. Overseen by the self-regulating Entertainment Software Rating Board (ESRB), this system rates games on the basis of sexual and violent content, with M-rated, or Mature, games being ones that should not be sold to children under the age of seventeen without a parent physically present at the point of sale. However, many parents ignore, do not fully understand, or do not care about the ratings, so this system has done little to prevent younger children from playing violent games.

Early Laws

Because children were still gaining access to violent games despite the ESRB, some city and state officials decided to pass laws that limited this access. Among the first were a 2000 Indianapolis law that prohibited minors—defined in the state as children under eighteen—from

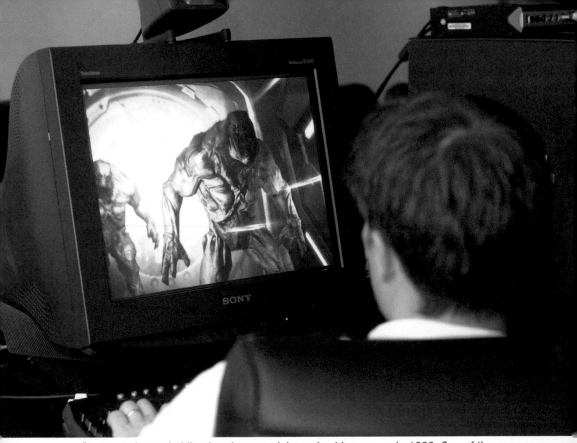

Congress began holding hearings on violence in video games in 1993. One of the games that drew criticism was Doom. *A later version of the game appears here.*

playing or viewing violent games in arcades, and a 2002 St. Louis, Missouri, law that prohibited children under seventeen from playing violent games in arcades and prohibited anyone from selling or renting a violent game to a minor. Both laws were struck down by federal courts that deemed them infringements on the US right to freedom of expression.

The first state law met a similar fate. Passed in Washington State in May 2003, this law would have prevented anyone from selling a child under eighteen a video game that contained "realistic or photographic-like depictions of aggressive conflict"[58] against law enforcement officers and/or firefighters. However, federal judge Robert Lasnik issued an injunction against the law going into effect while the question of whether it violated free speech was considered. Ultimately, Lasnik ruled the law unconstitutional because it was both too narrow and too broad—too narrow for banning violence against police and firefighters but not others, and too broad for not limiting its protections to real-world heroes as opposed to evil, tyrannical police officers, space-alien police officers, or cartoon figures.

In noting this problem, Lasnik said, "Would a game built around 'The Simpsons' or the 'Looney Tunes' characters be 'realistic' enough to trigger the act? The real problem is that [a store] clerk might know everything there is to know about the game and yet not be able to determine whether it can legally be sold to a minor."[59] Worries about satisfying the requirements of the law, Lasnik suggested, might lead both sales clerks and game manufacturers to be overly cautious in what they provided to the public, and this could negatively impact free speech.

More Attempts

Such decisions did little to curtail lawmakers' efforts to enact laws restricting video game sales, especially after the public learned in 2005 that by installing a mod (short for *modification*, an alteration of the program code of a video game) found online into *Grand Theft Auto: San Andreas*, players could access an otherwise hidden sexually explicit minigame. The company that manufactured the game insisted that computer hackers were entirely responsible for this sexual content, whereas the mod's creators said they had merely unlocked a minigame that was already there. Many gamers have speculated that the company initially intended for this minigame to be a part of the original game but decided it was too explicit and locked it away from players—an easier fix than removing it from the program code.

In either case, the revelation that a game could have hidden content or develop new content after it had already been rated by the ESRB caused a great deal of outrage. In response, the ESRB changed the game's rating from Mature to Adults Only. Then-senator Hillary Clinton called on the Federal Trade Commission to investigate who was responsible for the mod in order to determine whether advertisements for the game had intentionally misrepresented its content. Clinton also stressed the need to find legislative solutions to keep children from having access to sexually explicit and/or violent video game content.

Depicting Legal Punishments

Opponents of violent gaming have complained that violent video games often show crimes without also showing the legal consequences of those crimes. This, they say, might lead gamers to think that they can commit violent acts in real life without repercussions. Consequently, some people have called on game manufacturers to include more punishments in their games. For example, the International Committee of the Red Cross (ICRC) has pushed for video games to punish crimes committed in battle in the same ways that such war crimes would be punished in real life. On its website the organization states,

> As in real life, these games [those simulating real-life war situations] should include virtual consequences for people's actions and decisions. . . . The ICRC is concerned that certain game scenarios could lead to a trivialization of serious violations of the law of armed conflict. The fear is that eventually such illegal acts will be perceived as acceptable behaviour.

As ICRC spokesperson Bernard Barrett clarifies,

> We're not asking for censorship, we don't want to take any elements out of the games. We're not trying to make games boring or preachy, but we're hoping that the ones that offer a realistic portrayal of a modern battlefield can incorporate some sort of reward or penalties depending on whether they follow the basic rules of armed conflict. We are not talking about censorship or banning anything. It's just making it more realistic, the same way the military has rules on the battlefield, then gamers have the same rules.

International Committee of the Red Cross, "Video Games and Law of War," September 27, 2013. www.icrc.org.

Quoted in Henry Austin, "War Crimes in Video Games Should Be Punished, ICRC Says," NBC News, October 3, 2013. www.nbcnews.com.

A California Appeal

Amidst these developments, several states passed laws restricting children's access to video games, but these statutes were ruled unconstitutional. One of these rulings, however, was appealed all the way to the US Supreme Court. The legislation in question, passed in California and signed into law in 2005 by then-governor Arnold Schwarzenegger, banned the sale of violent video games to children under eighteen. It defined violent video games as games featuring "killing, maiming, dismembering, or sexually assaulting an image of a human being" that possessed "substantially human characteristics"[60] specifically because viewing such images could cause psychological harm and make it more likely for young people to behave in aggressive or antisocial ways. The law also imposed a $1,000 fine on violators.

Even before the law went into effect, the gaming industry was working to overturn it. Two industry representatives, the Entertainment Merchants Association and the Entertainment Software Association, sued the state of California. They argued that the ban was unconstitutional based on the First Amendment, which protects free speech, and the Fourteenth Amendment, which prohibits states from passing or enforcing laws that violate a US citizen's constitutional rights. But during the resulting trial, lawyers for California focused not on rights but on the harm that the state believed video games could do, saying that this harm was severe enough to justify a restriction on freedom of speech. Courts have found this argument compelling in other situations; for example, a person does not have the right to yell "Fire!" as a prank in a crowded theater because audience members could get seriously hurt while running to the exits.

To prove their case, California's lawyers presented evidence from psychologists and other experts who had done research suggesting that violent video games caused violent behavior and psychological problems. It also showed particularly violent scenes from video games, including *Grand Theft Auto: Vice City* and *Duke Nukem 3D*. Nonetheless, the court still found that the law violated the First Amendment. California appealed the decision, but the next court to hear the case, the US Court of Appeals for the Ninth District, also found that the law was unconstitutional. However, in issuing this decision in 2007, the court acknowledged that the state had a right to protect minors. It just did not believe that there was enough proof that playing video games could harm children.

Protesters rally on the steps of the Supreme Court Building prior to 2011 hearings on California's proposed ban on violent video games.

A Supreme Court Decision

After this ruling California asked the US Supreme Court to review the case, and in 2010 the Court decided to do so. In 2011, after completing its review, the Court allowed the Ninth Circuit ruling to stand. In making this decision, with a vote of seven to two, members of the Court referenced an earlier 2011 Court decision that struck down a federal law making it a crime to sell videos depicting animal cruelty. The reasoning in that case was that one category of speech should not be set apart from others and given fewer protections than the rest.

The Court also questioned how one would be able to judge which video games would qualify as being worthy of banning. Justice Antonin Scalia asked California's attorneys how a person would determine what constituted a "normal" level of violence, for example. He also expressed concern that such judgments might eventually be applied to books as well, saying, "Some of the Grimm's fairy tales are quite grim. Are you going to ban them too?"[61]

But Justice Stephen G. Breyer countered that common sense dictates that the government should be able to prevent young people from having access to images that most members of a civilized society can agree are repugnant. He noted that the Court had already done this with one category of speech: the sexually explicit. In 1968 the Court upheld the government's right to regulate the distribution of sexual materials to minors, and in 1973 it declared that obscenity was not protected by the First Amendment and provided guidelines for determining what constituted obscene content. Breyer felt this should have been done with video games as well. In a dissent to the Court's finding in the 2011 California case, he wrote,

> "What kind of First Amendment would permit the government to protect children by restricting sales of that extremely violent video game only when the woman—bound, gagged, tortured, and killed—is also topless?"[62]
>
> —US Supreme Court justice Stephen Breyer.

What sense does it make to forbid selling to a 13-year-old boy a magazine with an image of a nude woman while protecting a sale to that 13-year-old of an interactive video game in which he actively, but virtually, binds and gags the woman, then tortures and kills her? What kind of First Amendment would permit the government to protect children by restricting sales of that extremely violent video game only when the woman—bound, gagged, tortured, and killed—is also topless?[62]

Flawed Studies

The Court also dealt a blow to advocates for a ban on violent video games by dismissing as flawed all studies suggesting there might be a link between playing violent games and engaging in violent acts. The Court stated,

Psychological studies purporting to show a connection between exposure to violent video games and harmful effects on children do not prove that such exposure causes minors to act aggressively. Any demonstrated effects are both small and indistinguishable from effects produced by other media. Since California has declined to restrict those other media, e.g., Saturday morning cartoons, its video-game regulation is wildly underinclusive, raising serious doubts about whether the State is pursuing the interest it invokes or is instead disfavoring a particular speaker or viewpoint.[63]

The justices also seemed to suggest that violent video games have literary and/or artistic value. This is significant because one of the Court's criteria for determining whether obscene material can be banned is that it lacks such value. To the Court, the fact that video games have characters, dialogue, and other elements similar to those in books and movies means they are equivalent to books and movies. Therefore, according to Justice Scalia, although reading great literature is "unquestionably more cultured and intellectually edifying than playing Mortal Kombat, . . . crudely violent video games, tawdry TV shows, and cheap novels and magazines are no less forms of speech"[64] than great literature and are therefore just as deserving of First Amendment protection.

Breyer, however, expressed concern that the Court's decision would mean merchants could sell violent games directly to children without parents being involved. Indeed, in the years since the Court's decision, some merchants, especially in California, are hesitant even to call customers' attention to the ESRB's age ratings that appear on game packaging. This has increased the number of parents making purchases without being aware of a game's content.

In addition, the Court's position that research linking violent gaming to violent acts is flawed has led many parents to believe that there is nothing wrong with allowing their children to play violent games. Jurgen Freund, who has studied this issue in the United Kingdom, which has a ratings system similar to the one in the United States, reports, "Most parents think their child is mature enough so that these games will not influ-

"Most parents think their child is mature enough so that these games will not influence them."[65]

—Jurgen Freund, a UK expert on the effect of violent games on children.

ence them."[65] Freund's research has also shown that most parents do not bother to review the latest games their children are asking to play to determine their content.

Other Approaches

Despite the fact that many laws attempting to restrict access to violent video games have been overturned, some lawmakers continue to propose new laws addressing the same problem. For example, in 2013 Governor Chris Christie of New Jersey convened a task force to study violence in gaming and proposed a new law in his state that would ban retailers from selling M-rated games to minors without a parent's permission. Given the Supreme Court 2011 ruling on California's similar ban on sales to minors, many legal scholars have said that Christie's proposed law would have little chance of withstanding challenges to its constitutionality.

In 2013 New Jersey governor Chris Christie proposed a law banning the sale of M-rated games to minors. Many legal experts believe the bill will be overturned in the courts for violating First Amendment rights.

"Too Far a Leap"

Perhaps the first attempt to hold a video game company legally responsible for a mass shooting was a lawsuit filed in 1997 by attorney Jack Thompson on behalf of the parents of three children killed in a shooting at Heath High School in West Paducah, Kentucky. The shooter, fourteen-year-old Michael Carneal, had spent many hours playing violent video games that included *Doom, Mortal Kombat,* and *Castle Wolfenstein.* Thompson sued the manufacturers of the video games Carneal played as well as the operators of the pornographic websites the young man had visited and the producers of a movie that Carneal owned in which a student fantasizes about committing a school shooting. Thompson sought $33 million in damages for the victims' families, but in 2001, after many court proceedings, the US Court of Appeals for the Sixth Circuit ruled that it was "simply too far a leap from shooting characters on a video screen to shooting people in a classroom" and dismissed the case.

Mike Jaccarino, "'Training Simulation': Mass Killers Often Share Obsession with Violent Video Games," Fox News, September 12, 2013. www.foxnews.com.

Nonetheless, opponents of violent video games say it is important to keep trying to enact bans on such games. One such opponent is New Jersey assemblyman Sean Kean, who proposed his own law separate from Christie's that would fine retailers who sell an M-rated video game to a child without parental permission. Kean admits that his proposed law and similar ones would face legal challenges, but he suggests that every new mass shooting, such as the one at Sandy Hook Elementary, might cause judges to change their minds regarding the need for bans. Kean stresses that it is important to keep putting such laws in front of judges, as he explains: "I think it's one of these cases where if we continue to push then maybe we can get some common sense coming out of the court."[66] Others express the hope that bans against excessively violent games in other countries—such as Australia, New Zealand, Germany, and Brazil—will show US judges that eliminating access to such games does not harm the public.

But other opponents of violent gaming doubt the courts will change their minds on game bans. Consequently, some are proposing alternative approaches to reducing or even eliminating the availability of such games. For example, in February 2014 the US Republican Party suggested a tax reform that would exclude the creators of violent video games from receiving a research-and-development tax credit that other US companies receive to offset expenses related to creating new products and technologies. In commenting on this strategy, gaming expert Nathan Grayson says that it gets around

> the tricky issue of games qualifying for first amendment—aka, freedom of speech—protection in a *specific case* involving government regulation of violent videogames. This would essentially function as a way of tip-toeing around that. The government wouldn't be passing judgment by levying a new tax; it would just be withholding a tax *break*. Sneaky, sneaky. [67]

Societal Pressures

Others have suggested that the way to stop companies from creating violent games is to sue them every time such a game appears to have been connected to a crime. Former attorney Jack Thompson, for example, has taken this approach, suing on behalf of people who have lost family members to violence that Thompson believes was ultimately the result of playing violent video games. However, his efforts have been unsuccessful, and Paul Smith, an attorney who specializes in First Amendment issues and has represented video game companies in court, says that such efforts will likely always fail because they threaten First Amendment rights. As Smith explains, "If you start saying that we're going to sue people because one individual out there read their book or played their game and decided to become a criminal, there is no stopping point."[68] This, he suggests, could lead to widespread censorship—something the courts would not allow.

Some people say a better approach is to rely on societal pressure to make violent gaming unattractive. This might take some time to

"If you start saying that we're going to sue people because one individual out there read their book or played their game and decided to become a criminal, there is no stopping point."[68]

—Paul Smith, an attorney who specializes in First Amendment issues.

work, but in the end it could lead a new generation to consider gaming harmful rather than fun. Dave Grossman notes that this has happened with other behaviors that society once accepted but now rejects:

> Today we have the moral courage to tell someone, "Don't you dare get in that car in this drunken state. I am going to call you a taxi." We have achieved a moral outrage about drunken drivers, and drunks are now modifying their behaviour because of this moral outrage. Similarly we now say, "I'd rather you didn't light up a cigarette, please. This is a non-smoking area." When we have the moral courage to get up and say so, then we have achieved a moral indignation that truly modifies a smoker's behaviour. In the same way, we need to say to kids about violent games, "That's sick."[69]

"We need to say to kids about violent games, 'That's sick.'"[69]

—Dave Grossman, a retired US Army lieutenant colonel and expert on violent gaming.

Given how popular violent games are, however, some people say it is unlikely that this kind of social pressure will come to bear. Indeed, some of the most popular video games are the violent ones. For example, in February 2014 the makers of *Grand Theft Auto V* reported that between the time this game was released on September 17, 2013, and the end of that year, they sold 32.5 million copies of it, making it the best selling game of 2013. This sales figure suggests that many people do not believe playing violent video games is harmful and would not support efforts, legal or otherwise, to curtail an activity they find enjoyable.

Source Notes

Introduction: Compelling Violence

1. Quoted in Matt Homan, "Ohio State Professor: Violent Games Can Make Players More Aggressive," *Lantern*, February 6, 2014. http://thelantern.com.

2. Quoted in Maria Konnikova, "Why Gamers Can't Stop Playing First-Person Shooters," *Elements* (blog), November 26, 2013. www.newyorker.com.

3. Steve Tilley, "*Titanfall* Review: Multiplayer First-Person Shooter Will Get You Addicted," *Toronto Sun*, March 10, 2014. www.torontosun.com.

4. Quoted in Homan, "Ohio State Professor."

Chapter One: Video Games and Mass Shootings

5. Quoted in Helen Pidd, "Anders Breivik 'Trained' for Shooting Attacks by Playing *Call of Duty*," *Guardian*, April 19, 2012. www.guardian.co.uk.

6. Quoted in Pidd, "Anders Breivik 'Trained' for Shooting Attacks by Playing *Call of Duty*."

7. Quoted in Tom Law, "Anders Breivik: Did *Call of Duty* Really Influence the Norway Massacre?," *Sabotage Times*. www.sabotagetimes.com.

8. Law, "Anders Breivik."

9. Paul Tassi, "The Idiocy of Blaming Video Games for the Norway Massacre," *Forbes*, April 19, 2012. www.forbes.com.

10. Dave Grossman, "Teaching Kids to Kill," *Phi Kappa Phi National Forum*, Fall 2000. www.killology.com.

11. Quoted in Jeff Grabmeier, "Video Games Can Teach How to Shoot Guns More Accurately and Aim for the Head," Ohio State University Research and Innovations Communications, April 30, 2012. http://researchnews.osu.edu.

12. Quoted in Grabmeier, "Video Games Can Teach How to Shoot Guns More Accurately and Aim for the Head."

13. Grossman, "Teaching Kids to Kill."

14. Grossman, "Teaching Kids to Kill."

15. Dave Grossman, "The Violent Video Game Plague," *Knowledge of Reality*. www.sol.com.au/kor/17_03.htm.

16. Christopher J. Ferguson, "Don't Link Video Games with Mass Shootings," CNN, September 20, 2013. www.cnn.com.

17. Ferguson, "Don't Link Video Games with Mass Shootings."

18. Matt Peckham, "Norway Killer Played *World of Warcraft*, Which Probably Means Nothing at All," *Time*, April 17, 2012. http://techland.time.com.

19. Peckham, "Norway Killer Played *World of Warcraft*, Which Probably Means Nothing at All."

20. Tassi, "The Idiocy of Blaming Video Games for the Norway Massacre."

21. Quoted in Daniel Beekman, "NRA Blames Video Games Like 'Kindergarten Killer' for Sandy Hook Elementary Slaughter," *New York Daily News*, December 21, 2012. www.nydailynews.com.

22. Quoted in Beekman, "NRA Blames Video Games Like 'Kindergarten Killer' for Sandy Hook Elementary Slaughter."

23. Max Fisher, "Ten Country Comparison Suggests There's No Link Between Video Games and Gun Murders," *WorldViews* (blog), December 17, 2012. www.washingtonpost.com.

24. Quoted in Beekman, "NRA Blames Video Games Like 'Kindergarten Killer' for Sandy Hook Elementary Slaughter."

25. Tobias Greitemeyer and Dirk O. Mugge, "Video Games Do Affect Social Outcomes," *Sage Journals*, July 11, 2013. http://psp.sagepub.com.

26. Jean M. Twenge, "Yes, Violent Video Games Do Cause Aggression," *Our Changing Culture* (blog), December 21, 2012. www.psychologytoday.com.

27. Christopher J. Ferguson, "Video Games Don't Make Kids Violent," *Time*, December 7, 2011. http://ideas.time.com.

28. Quoted in Devin Coldewey, "Video Gamers' Aggression Born from Frustration, Not Violence: Study," NBC News, April 8, 2014. www.nbcnews.com.

29. Jesse Fox, Jeremy N. Bailenson, and Liz Tricase, "The Embodiment of Sexualized Virtual Selves: The Proteus Effect and Experiences of Self-Objectification via Avatars," *Computers in Human Behavior*, vol. 29, 2013, pp. 930–38. http://vhil.stanford.edu.

30. Joseph Bernstein, "The Scientific Connection Between Sexist Video Games and Rape Culture," BuzzFeed, October 23, 2013. www.buzzfeed.com.

31. Quoted in Owen S. Good, "Study Suggests Playing as a Black Character Can Reinforce Racist Attitudes," Polygon, March 22, 2014. www.polygon.com.

32. Quoted in Good, "Study Suggests Playing as a Black Character Can Reinforce Racist Attitudes."

33. Quoted in Ben Kuchera, "Video Games, Racism, and Violence: The Problems Behind the Science 'Proving' They're Linked," Polygon, March 27, 2014. www.polygon.com.

34. Quoted in Kuchera, "Video Games, Racism, and Violence."

35. Quoted in Kuchera, "Video Games, Racism, and Violence."

36. Quoted in Rebecca Leung, "Can a Video Game Lead to Murder?," *60 Minutes*, February 9, 2005. www.cbsnews.com.

37. Tom Jacobs, "Violent Video Games and Bad Behavior: The Evidence Mounts," *Pacific Standard*, February 10, 2014. www.psmag.com.

38. Quoted in Mike Lupica, "Morbid Find Suggests Murder-Obsessed Gunman Adam Lanza Plotted Newtown, Conn.'s Sandy Hook Massacre for Years," *New York Daily News*, March 17, 2013. www.nydailynews.com.

39. Quoted in Hannah Schwarz and Marek Ramilo, "Sandy Hook Shooter Treated at Yale," *Yale Daily News*, January 22, 2014. http://yaledailynews.com.

40. Quoted in Schwarz and Ramilo, "Sandy Hook Shooter Treated at Yale."

41. Quoted in Phil Owen, "Do Video Games Make Depression Worse?," Kotaku, November 26, 2012. http://kotaku.com.

42. Quoted in Owen, "Do Video Games Make Depression Worse?"

43. Henry Jenkins, "Reality Bytes: Eight Myths About Video Games Debunked," *Video Game Revolution*, PBS. www.pbs.org.

44. Quoted in Michael Abbott, "In Praise of Empathy and Good Teaching," *Brainy Gamer* (blog), October 19, 2007. www.brainy gamer.com.

45. Abbott, "In Praise of Empathy and Good Teaching."

46. Dennis Scimeca, "I'm Mentally Ill, I Love Violent Video Games, and They've Never Made Me Feel Like Killing Anyone," Kotaku, January 16, 2013. http://kotaku.com.

47. Scimeca, "I'm Mentally Ill, I Love Violent Video Games, and They've Never Made Me Feel Like Killing Anyone."

48. Quoted in Serena Gordon, "Video Game 'Addiction' Tied to Depression, Anxiety in Kids," Health Day, January 17, 2011. http://health.usnews.com.

49. Quoted in *Talk of the Nation*, "Compulsive Video Gaming: Addiction or Vice?," NPR, July 10, 2007. www.wbur.org.

50. Quoted in *Talk of the Nation*, "Compulsive Video Gaming."

51. Quoted in Kaylee Remington, "Petric Appears on Katie Couric," *Morning Journal News*, May 2, 2013. www.morningjournal.com.

52. Paul Runge, "Video Games Represent the Most Powerful (and Potentially Dangerous) Era in Storytelling," *Huffington Post*, October 21, 2013. www.huffingtonpost.com.

53. Quoted in Tamara Lush, "At War with *World of Warcraft*: An Addict Tells His Story," *Guardian*, August 29, 2011. www.theguardian.com.

54. Quoted in Gregg Toppo, "10 Years Later, the Real Story Behind Columbine," *USA Today*, April 14, 2009. www.usatoday.com.

55. Quoted in Mike Jaccarino, "'Frag Him': Video Games Ratchet Up Violence, Blur Line Between Fantasy and Reality," Fox News, September 13, 2013. www.foxnews.com.

Chapter Four: Legal Responses to Gaming Issues

56. Quoted in Ryan Lambie, "*Night Trap*: A Closer Look at One of the Most Controversial Games Ever Made," Den of Geek, January 23, 2012. www.denofgeek.us.

57. Quoted in Dan Seitz, "Another Anti–Video Game Foe Is Out of Power: Joe Lieberman Is No Longer a Senator," Uproxx, January 4, 2013. http://uproxx.com.

58. Quoted in Fred Locklear, "Judge Strikes Down Washington State's Violent Video Game Law," Ars Technica, July 15, 2004. http://arstechnica.com.

59. Quoted in Locklear, "Judge Strikes Down Washington State's Violent Video Game Law."

60. Quoted in Legal Information Institute, "*Schwarzenegger v. Entertainment Merchants Association*," Cornell University Law School. www.law.cornell.edu.

61. Quoted in Adam Liptak, "Justices Debate Video Game Ban," *New York Times*, November 2, 2010. www.nytimes.com.

62. Quoted in Joan Biskupic and Mike Snider, "Supreme Court Rejects Ban on Violent Video Games," *USA Today*, June 28, 2011. www.usatoday.com.

63. Quoted in Evan Narcisse, "Supreme Court: 'Video Games Qualify for First Amendment Protection,'" *Time*, June 27, 2011. http://techland.time.com.

64. Quoted in Narcisse, "Supreme Court."

65. Quoted in Alfred Hermida, "Parents 'Ignore Game Age Ratings,'" BBC News, June 24, 2005. http://news.bbc.co.uk.

66. Quoted in Game Politics, "Experts: Chris Christie's Video Game Proposals Would Face Uphill Legal Battles," April 24, 2013. www.gamepolitics.com.

67. Nathan Grayson, "US Tax Plan Singles Out Makers of 'Violent Videogames,'" Rock, Paper, Shotgun, February 28, 2014. www.rockpapershotgun.com.

68. Quoted in Leung, "Can a Video Game Lead to Murder?"

69. Grossman, "The Violent Video Game Plague."

American Civil Liberties Union (ACLU)

125 Broad St., 18th Floor
New York, NY 10004
phone: (212) 549-2500
e-mail: aclu@aclu.org
website: www.aclu.org

An opponent of government efforts to censor books, movies, video games, and other forms of media, the ACLU has been involved in many legal cases related to First Amendment rights.

Ars Technica

website: http://arstechnica.com

The Ars Technica website provides articles about video gaming, technology, and Internet issues.

Center for Internet and Technology Addiction

17 S. Highland St.
West Hartford, CT 06119
phone: (860) 561-8727
e-mail: drdave@virtual-addiction.com
website: www.virtual-addiction.com

The Center for Internet and Technology Addiction provides counseling, information, and resources related to online addictions. Its website offers articles, news releases, and videos related to these addictions.

Entertainment Software Association (ESA)

575 Seventh St. NW, Suite 300
Washington, DC 20004
e-mail: esa@theesa.com
website: www.theesa.com

A trade association representing companies that publish and market video games, the ESA has been involved in legal efforts to fight the censorship of games and the restriction of their sale to minors.

Entertainment Software Rating Board (ESRB)

317 Madison Ave., 22nd Floor
New York, NY 10017
phone: (212) 759-0700
e-mail: info@esrb.org
website: www.esrb.org

Established by the Entertainment Software Association, the ESRB oversees the voluntary ratings system whereby parents can determine which video games are appropriate for their children. The association's website also provides information about these ratings and the criteria the board uses to determine them.

Federal Trade Commission (FTC)

600 Pennsylvania Ave. NW
Washington, DC 20580
phone: (202) 326-2222
website: www.ftc.gov

Charged with protecting consumers, the FTC is involved in issues related to the purchase and playing of video games. Its website includes articles on video game ratings and video game violence.

Game Politics

website: www.gamepolitics.com

The Game Politics website, subtitled "Where Politics and Games Collide," provides information about political issues related to video gaming.

Mental Illness Policy Organization

50 E. 129th St., Suite PH7
New York, NY 10035
e-mail: office@mentalillnesspolicy.org
website: http://mentalillnesspolicy.org

A nonprofit organization, the Mental Illness Policy Organization provides information on serious mental illnesses, violence, involuntary treatment, hospitalization, and other issues related to mental health and violence. Its website links to numerous articles on subjects related to mental illness issues.

Books

Andrew P. Doan and Brooke Strickland, *Hooked on Games: The Lure and Cost of Video Game and Internet Addiction.* Coralville, IA: FEP International, 2012.

Christopher J. Ferguson, *Adolescents, Crime, and the Media.* New York: Springer Science+Business Media, 2013.

Kishonna L. Gray, *Race, Gender, and Deviance in Xbox Live.* Waltham, MA: Anderson, 2014.

Dave Grossman and Gloria DeGaetano, *Stop Teaching Our Kids to Kill.* New York: Harmony, 2014.

Frank E. Hagan, *Introduction to Criminology.* Thousand Oaks, CA: Sage, 2011.

David Kushner, *Jacked: The Outlaw Story of "Grand Theft Auto."* Hoboken, NJ: Wiley, 2012.

Peter Langman, *Why Kids Kill: Inside the Mind of School Shooters.* New York: Palgrave Macmillan, 2009.

Fletcher Wortmann, *Triggered: A Memoir of Obsessive-Compulsive Disorder.* New York: Thomas Dunn, 2012.

Internet Sources

Doug Gross, "The 10 Most Controversial Violent Video Games," CNN, August 26, 2013. www.cnn.com/2013/08/26/tech/gaming -gadgets/controversial-violent-video-games.

Tom Hawking, "Game Never Over: The Ten Most Addictive Video Games," *Rolling Stone.* www.rollingstone.com/culture/pictures /game-never-over-10-most-addictive-video-games-20140311.

Index

Picture Credits

About the Author

Patricia D. Netzley has written more than fifty books for children, teens, and adults. She has also worked as an editor, a writing instructor, and a knitting teacher. She is a member of the Society of Children's Book Writers and Illustrators.